First World War
and Army of Occupation
War Diary
France, Belgium and Germany

59 DIVISION
Divisional Troops
Machine Gun Corps
59 Battalion
1 March 1918 - 30 April 1918

WO95/3017/11

The Naval & Military Press Ltd
www.nmarchive.com
Published in association with The National Archives

Published by

The Naval & Military Press Ltd

Unit 10 Ridgewood Industrial Park,

Uckfield, East Sussex,

TN22 5QE England

Tel: +44 (0) 1825 749494

www.naval-military-press.com

www.nmarchive.com

This diary has been reprinted in facsimile from the original. Any imperfections are inevitably reproduced and the quality may fall short of modern type and cartographic standards.

© **Crown Copyright**
Images reproduced by permission of The National Archives, London, England, 2015.

Contents

Document type	Place/Title	Date From	Date To
Heading	WO95/3017/11		
Heading	59 Division Div Troops 59 BN Machine Gun Corps 1918 Mar-Apr		
Heading	59th Divisional M.G.C. War Diary 59th Battalion Machine Gun Corps March 1918 Attached:- Report On Operation Orders.		
Heading	59th Bn Machine Gun Corps War Diary For The Month Of March 1918 Volume I		
War Diary	Mory Refee Sheet Lens II.1/100000	01/03/1918	22/03/1918
War Diary	Courcelles-Le Comte Refee Lens Sheet II 1/100000	23/03/1918	23/03/1918
War Diary	Ablainleville	23/03/1918	23/03/1918
War Diary	Miraumont Ref Sheet Lens II 1/100000	23/03/1918	23/03/1918
War Diary	Bouzincourt Ref Sheet Len II 1/100000	24/03/1918	26/03/1918
War Diary	Bonneville	27/03/1918	27/03/1918
War Diary	Candas	28/03/1918	28/03/1918
War Diary	Frevillers.	29/03/1918	29/03/1918
War Diary	Villers Brulin	31/03/1918	31/03/1918
Heading	59th Divisional Troops 59th Battalion Machine Gun Corps March 1918 Reports On Operations Attached		
Miscellaneous	59th Battn. Machine Gun Corps.	21/03/1918	21/03/1918
Miscellaneous	59th Battn. Machine Gun Corps	21/03/1918	21/03/1918
Miscellaneous	Appendix 1		
Operation(al) Order(s)	59th Batt M.G. Corps Operation Order No. 2	25/03/1918	25/03/1918
Operation(al) Order(s)	59th Batt M.G. Corps Operation Order No. 4.		
Heading	War Diary 59th Battn Machine Gun Corps April 1918		
War Diary	Villers Brulin (Sheet Lens II 1/100000)	01/04/1918	01/04/1918
War Diary	Sheet Hazebrouck. 5.a 1/100000	02/04/1918	05/04/1918
War Diary	Sheet 27/favce And Belgium 1/40000	06/04/1918	07/04/1918
War Diary	Zonnebeke 1/10000	08/04/1918	08/04/1918
War Diary	Sheet 28 (Belgium)1/40000	10/04/1918	13/04/1918
War Diary	Locre Raj Sheet 28 Belgium 1/40000	14/04/1918	25/04/1918
War Diary	Herzelle	26/04/1918	30/04/1918
Heading	59th Divisional Troops 59th Battalion Machine Gun Corps April 1918 Report On Operations Attached		
Miscellaneous	Appendix I. Machine Gun Defence	05/04/1918	05/04/1918
Miscellaneous	59th Batt Machine Gun Corps	13/04/1918	13/04/1918
Miscellaneous	Lessons Learnt		
Operation(al) Order(s)	59th Batt Machine Gun Corps Operation Order No. 5	31/03/1918	31/03/1918
Miscellaneous	Instruction		
Operation(al) Order(s)	59th Batt Machine Gun Corps Operation Order No. 6	03/04/1918	03/04/1918
Operation(al) Order(s)	59th Batt Machine Gun Corps Operation Order No 7	08/04/1918	08/04/1918
Operation(al) Order(s)	59th Battn M.G.C. Warning Order No. 1	12/04/1918	12/04/1918
Operation(al) Order(s)	59th Bn M.G.C. Operation Order No. 8	12/04/1918	12/04/1918
Operation(al) Order(s)	59th Batt Machine Gun Corps Operation Order No 9.	21/04/1918	21/04/1918
Operation(al) Order(s)	59th Bn M.G.C. Order No. 10 Appendix 7	26/04/1918	26/04/1918
Miscellaneous	59th Bn. M.G. Corps.	01/05/1918	01/05/1918

3095 3017/11

59 DIVISION
ON TROOPS

59 BN Machine Gun Corps

1918 MAR — APR

59th Divisional M.G.C.

| WAR DIARY |

59th BATTALION

MACHINE GUN CORPS

MARCH 1918

Attached :- Report on Operations.

Operation Orders.

59 to 59 Div

Original

Vol I

59th Bn Machine Gun Corps

War Diary
for the
month of March 1918

Pages 1 to 6

Volume I

Army Form C. 2118.

Page 1

WAR DIARY
or
INTELLIGENCE SUMMARY.
(Erase heading not required.)

Instructions regarding War Diaries and Intelligence Summaries are contained in F. S. Regs., Part II. and the Staff Manual respectively. Title pages will be prepared in manuscript.

Place	Date	Hour	Summary of Events and Information	Remarks and references to Appendices
MORY After Shut Known Yseron	1.3.17		Orders having been received that the 4 Machine Gun Companies in the Division were to be incorporated into the 89th Battalion Machine Gun Corps, on the going out of the line, the 177 and 200 Machine Gun Companies went to two our and Battalion Headquarters were established at Durrow camp MORY. The 177 Machine Gun Company became "B" company, 200 Machine Gun company became "D" company. The two Machine Gun companies were covering the Divisional Front, one leg in the Right Sector and one leg in the Left Sector, two companies in reserve at DURROW CAMP. The officers in distribution Headquarters at this date are shown in Appendix 1. D company relieved 197 Machine Gun company in the right sector of the Divisional Front.	
	5.3.17		The 197 Machine Gun Company having moved out of the line during the night of 7/5th were incorporated into the Battalion and became "A" Company. C Company relieved 195 Machine Gun Company in the Left Sector of the Divisional Front.	
	9.3.17		195 Machine Gun Company having moved out of the line was incorporated into the Battalion and became "J" Company. A practice S.O.S. having on the Divisional front was fired down by the two companies in the front line between 5.5 p.m. and 5.15 p.m.	

Army Form C. 2118.

Page II

WAR DIARY
or
INTELLIGENCE SUMMARY.
(Erase heading not required.)

Place	Date	Hour	Summary of Events and Information	Remarks and references to Appendices
	11.3.16		Orders received from Divisional Headquarters for all Machine Gun positions (including loopholes) to be manned after dusk on evening of 12th March. Instructions were accordingly issued to B Company to reinforce all "B" positions and A Company to occupy the positions of A and C Batteries. There 8 gun Battery positions were each and camouflaged by A Company. These were meant for the purpose of supporting a counter attack by the Reserve Brigade should the occasion arise.	
	12.3.16		The "B" positions and A and C Battery positions were reinforced at dusk by "B" and "A" Companies respectively. "C" Company moved to Ordnance Headquarters at c.3.05.55 "B" Company Headquarters took over huts the Company at Headquarters at MOST L'HOMME and "A" Company moved to Headquarters at B Battery.	
	13.3.16		Several dispositions were resumed on the line with the exception that machine gun teams remained at the "B" positions and the A and C Battery positions. Teams remained at the "B" positions and the A and C Battery positions returned to DURROW CAMP. "A" and "B" Company Headquarters returned to DURROW CAMP.	
	20.3.16		Orders received from Divisional Headquarters that the teams manning the gun positions in the first and second line system were to be issued to DINCE and to man and the remainder of the team return to DURROW CAMP.	

Army Form C. 2118.

Page III

WAR DIARY or INTELLIGENCE SUMMARY.
(Erase heading not required.)

Place	Date	Hour	Summary of Events and Information	Remarks and references to Appendices
	24.3.18		A heavy bombardment commenced on the south approach. At about 5.15 a Tp phone message was received from Division to send full strength team to man "B" position and A, B and C Batteries and to resume Battle positions. These orders were at once carried out and reports were soon received that positions were occupied.	
		10.15	A report from Advanced Battalion Headquarters that the enemy were in ECOUST and that parties had come had him out up to "C" Company to stand fast and that the guns in the "B" positions were standing by for target.	
		12.45	An aerial reconnaissance reported that the enemy were in ECOUST in large numbers and were forming up for attack. Orders were sent up to Advanced Battalion Headquarters to move the reserve section to a position to defend MORT L'HOMME.	
		15.0	Aeroplane of this wire reported and about the fact that the enemy were within 500 yards of MORT L'HOMME	
		16.0	Owing to the critical situation orders were sent to BURROW CAMP to form the 3rd etc. of the Machine Gun Battalion into a platoon and send them up as Infantry Reinforcements. This was accordingly done and by 17.45 the Officer Commanding "B" Company was in command of three platoons forming platoons at Cutting main.	
		21.30	Gun gun having been received from DADOS to replace those lost, these were sent up to Officer Commanding "A" Company together with two parties to remount it	

Army Form C. 2118.

Page II

WAR DIARY
or
INTELLIGENCE SUMMARY.
(Erase heading not required.)

Instructions regarding War Diaries and Intelligence Summaries are contained in F. S. Regs., Part II. and the Staff Manual respectively. Title pages will be prepared in manuscript.

Place	Date	Hour	Summary of Events and Information	Remarks and references to Appendices
	22.3.18	10.30	Orders were given for the Machine Gunners Batt. to be in the afternoon reinforcements to return to DURROW CAMP with the exception of 3a which were sent to A Company for reinforcement. Throughout the day messages the clearing of the battle zone occurred. Throughout the day the Battalion received reports that enemy attack, although at some distance that the German advanced their forward positions close to the 4th line. Scouts reported that the 2nd Division would take over from the 39th Division were informed that the 2nd Division would take over from the Division and that the garrison of the final line positions would assume under orders of the 2/2 Division. The situation was arranged and the Battalion at once under orders to officer commanding 2/2 Kn. Holm Machine Gun Coy and three companies "A" Company of every 2/2 mth and the General Battalion of commanding 4/2 Division.	
		3.0	The Details at DURROW CAMP (two companies) withdrew to COURCELLES LE COMTE. The transport were ordered to AFLAINZEVILLE.	
		9.0	Divisional Headquarters closed at REHAGNIES and D.M.G.C. opened his Battn H.Q. at COURCELLES LE COMTE.	
		22.0	A further report upon leaving here received from BAPES, two aeroplanes were engaged making up the details to meet them, on receipt of information, orders to the movement of the distribution of the Battalion (two coys - four guns) were issued to AFLAINZEVILLE.	
COURCELLES-LE-COMTE Ref: LENS SHEET	23.3.18	4.0.		

RBB

Army Form C. 2118.

Page V

WAR DIARY
or
INTELLIGENCE SUMMARY.
(Erase heading not required.)

Instructions regarding War Diaries and Intelligence Summaries are contained in F.S. Regs., Part II. and the Staff Manual respectively. Title pages will be prepared in manuscript.

Place	Date	Hour	Summary of Events and Information	Remarks and references to Appendices
ABLAINZEVILLE	23/3/17	4 a	Orders were received from Division that the Battalion must be prepared to move at MIRAUMONT at short notice.	
		7 a	Issued an Command of Battalion moved forward to reconnoitre the position over and in return reported the situation very critical. Positions were accordingly reconnoitred at ABLAINZEVILLE for the defence of the village and the two advanced sections this for its defence.	
		9 a	Orders received from the Division that the Battalion was to move at once by march route to BOUZINCOURT and that the remaining personnel would be transported by lorry at MIRAUMONT.	
		12.30	The transport moved off at 9.15 a.m. The lorries arrived and were ready to entrain at 12 p.m.	
MIRAUMONT Dir Sheet LENS 11 speech		17.30	at once to MIRAUMONT and the Battalion entrained at MIRAUMONT	
		18 o	Battalion detrained at AVELUY and marched to FUSILIER HUTS at AVELUY.	
BOUZINCOURT Big huts	24/3/17	19.30	BOUZINCOURT READ where situation was unchanged. Orders were received from Division that the Battalion was to be prepared to move to PONTAY and by march route during the night.	
LEN SU sheen	25/3/17	2.30	Battalion marched from FUSILIER HUTS and arrived at CONTAY by 6.30	
		19 30	Orders received from Division to report march route & East from CONTAY on the arrival of the afternoon of heath yesterday. See appendix	
		19 30	Orders received from Division that Battalion be prepared to move to CANDAS Area at short notice.	
	26/3/17 6.45		Battalion moved by march route to CANDAS area and were billeted on arrival at BONNEVILLE.	

Army Form C. 2118.

Page VI

WAR DIARY
or
INTELLIGENCE SUMMARY.
(Erase heading not required.)

Place	Date	Hour	Summary of Events and Information	Remarks and references to Appendices
BINNEVILLE	27.3.18		G.O.C. Division came over and congratulated Battalion on recent performance in battle.	
CANDAS	28.3.18	11.0	Transport moved by march route to BUSNES, and then on to HENIN-LE-SEC. Battalion entrained at CANDAS and detrained at LA PUGNOY where it was moved to FREVILLERS and were billeted for night.	
FREVILLERS	29.3.18		Battalion (less transport) marched to VILLERS BRULIN where it was accommodated in Billets.	
VILLERS BRULIN	29.3.18		Transport arrived during the day and were also billeted in the village.	
	31.3.18 11.15		Transport moved by march route to VILLERS.	
			Casualties to officers and other ranks in the battle from 21st were:	Appendix 4
			Officers killed one, wounded three, missing four.	
			Other Ranks killed one, wounded fifteen, missing three hundred and sixteen	
			An account of the battle from March 21st is given in Appendix 4.	
				F. Brisdon Lieut Col Commanding 5? Bn NF

59th Divisional Troops

59th BATTALION

MACHINE GUN CORPS

MARCH 1 9 1 8

Report on Operations attached.

59th Battn. Machine Gun Corps.

NOTES ON THE GERMAN ATTACK - MARCH 21st, 1918.

On March 3rd the Divisional Front was reduced and extended from 400 yds North of BULLECOURT to 400 yds North of the HIRONDELLE River, the reduced frontage being rather more than 4,000 yds.

The attack, which developed on March 21st, had been expected for some time, and the following measures had been taken to meet it.

1. Tunnellers had been used extensively to construct champagne emplacements. Though the programme was not carried out entirely most of the guns had shafts 20 ft deep by the 21st March.

2. A line of emplacements known as the "B" positions had been prepared about 3,000 yds behind the firing line. The construction of dug-outs for these positions had not commenced.

3. Carefully camouflaged champagne emplacements for 3 four-gun batteries had been prepared between 5,000 and 6,000 yds from our firing line.

4. Three 8-gun battery positions (X, Y & Z) had been dug and stocked with ammunition to support a counter-attack on the firing line of the 2nd system should this be necessary.

5. Emplacements were stocked with 15,000 rounds of S.A.A. per gun, an iron ration of oil, and water and rations for 48 hours.

6. Practice alarms were held every 48 hours an the times taken to get into position were reported to Battn H.Q. The teams were also practised in firing with Box Respirators.

7. A counter-preparation programme was drawn up to be used should an attack appear imminent. Not more than 5,000 rounds per gun were to be expended on counter-preparation and orders were given that no attempt should be made at long range fire should guns come under the hostile bombardment.

Dispositions.

The extent of the front made it impossible to cover the forward zone with short range M.G. fire with the guns available without sacrificing unduly the principle of defence in depth. Guns were therefore placed so as to protect the more important features, and, while this increased the chances of guns being dealt with in detail by the enemy, the front was defended to a depth of about 6,000 yds.

The 64 guns were disposed approximately as follows :-

```
Between  0 and  500 yds from the firing line  ...  ...  2 guns
   "    500  "  1000  "   "   "    "      "    ...  ... 12   "
   "   1000  "  2000  "   "   "    "      "    ...  ... 14   "
   "   2000  "  3000  "   "   "    "      "    ...  ...  8   "
   "   3000  "  4000  ("B" positions)          ...  ... 12   "
   "   5000  "  6000  ("A","B" & "C" Batteries      ... 12   "
In Reserve 8000 yds from the firing line       ...  ...  4   "
                                                         64  "
                                                        ========
```

The type of emplacement used was a small open emplacement designed to protect the gunners against any shelling except a direct hit. Most of the guns in the forward system were in trenches as sufficient time was not available to carry the spoil from dug-outs long distances. The emplacements of the "B" positions, which covered the Support line of the 2nd System were in carefully camouflaged pits, but dug-outs had not been constructed. "A", "B", & "C" Battery positions consisted of carefully camouflaged mined dug-outs with underground communication between the various guns.

A few days before the attack orders had been received to man the rear positions with nucleus teams.

As troops in the same Army had sustained casualties through prolonged gas bombardments the Corps issued orders on the 20th for gun teams to be reduced to 1 N.C.O. and 4 men in order that a relief might be available. This was done before the attack commenced.

At about 5 a.m. on the 21st the enemy commenced a heavy bombardment and at 5.30 orders were received from the Division to assume Battle Stations. The balance of the teams for the rear positions were galloped up in the limbers and the limbers returned at 7 a.m. without casualties.

The enemy maintained a heavy bombardment of gas shells and H.E. until shortly after 9, when his Infantry attacked. The main weight of the attack came up the NOREUIL Valley, the defence of which had been pulverised by the preliminary bombardment, the plan being to bomb up our support and reserve trenches at the same time as frontal attacks were being delivered.

Very little has been heard of the guns in the forward system, as survivors have only returned from four groups of guns.

The guns at 28a and 29a assuming an S.O.S. had gone up, opened fire on S.O.S. lines, as soon as the hostile bombardment commenced, until they were knocked out by shrapnel. While an effort was being made to repair the guns, the enemy advanced to within 30 yds of the gun position, and fire was opened on them with rifles and revolvers. The enemy were held up for some time and commenced an encircling movement. The teams then withdrew and did considerable further execution with a Lewis gun borrowed from the Artillery.

The guns 30a and 31a were destroyed by shell fire early in the action.

A survivor from 24a and 25a states that guns opened fire on S.O.S. lines when the bombardment commenced. About 9 a.m. the enemy appeared about 750 yds in front and advanced to within 200 yds of the guns. During this advance the survivor states that at least 1000 of the enemy were killed by M.G. fire. At 12.30 p.m. the guns were destroyed by shrapnel, and the teams withdrew to the dug-outs. They were then bombed from the back entrance by the enemy and the survivor escaped through the front entrance of the dug-out.

Guns Nos. 24 - 27 fired from 5 a.m. to 9 a.m. at slow rates on S.O.S. lines. At 9.10 a.m. information was received that the enemy had broken through and was making round the right flank. Guns were then mounted on the dug-out steps and fire was opened on the enemy. Maps and documents were destroyed. In the meantime the enemy had worked round to DEWSBURY Trench and had also begun to bomb up the RAILWAY RESERVE. Shortly afterwards the officer in charge gave orders to destroy the guns and withdraw. One man returned.

Guns Nos. 32 & 33 after inflicting about 100 casualties on the enemy at short range were bombed from the front and right. As their own bombs had been destroyed they could not reply and the Sergeant in charge gave orders to withdraw to RAILWAY RESERVE where the survivors fought as Infantry. Our troops in RAILWAY RESERVE were soon outnumbered and outflanked and an Infantry officer gave the order to withdraw.

No definite information has been received about other forward guns, though in several cases they were heard firing long after they were surrounded.

The line of the "B" positions was subjected to a heavy gas and H.E. bombardment from 5.30 a.m. onwards, but reports received at 11 a.m. show that only one gun had been destroyed and that the men were in good spirits and standing by for targets.

About noon the enemy were seen massing in ECOUST and shortly afterwards they resumed their advance. Their first attacks were checked by fire from the "B" position guns who bore the whole weight of the attack as no Infantry were available to garrison the support line 2nd System. Reports indicate that the first attack was defeated by M.G. fire, and that the enemy were driven back to ECOUST.

During this attack intense fire could be heard from guns Nos. 26b and 33b 27b Finally, however, the guns were surrounded and destroyed in detail. 2 signallers have returned from these gun teams

At 13.45 p.m. orders were received to move up the reserve section to a position to defend MORT HOMME

This was done and guns were in position about 2.30 p.m. At 3 p.m. the enemy reached the wire of the firing line 3rd System but his attack on this line was repulsed.

As the situation was critical 100 partially trained men of the M.G. Bn. were formed into platoons and sent up as Infantry to hold the line.

These men, together with a platoon of Artillerymen, worked as an Infantry Company under one of the Company Commanders, until the situation was restored by the arrival of the supporting Division.

Meanwhile the guns in "A","B", & "C" Batteries which had not been located by the hostile artillery had been engaging ideal targets. At about 1 p.m. dense masses of troops west of NOREUIL were seen from "A" Battery but the haze was so great that it was impossible to identify them. At 2000 yds range they were soon to be Germans and rapid fire was opened. Heavy casualties were caused but so great were their numbers that a large number succeeded in reaching the low ground near VRAUCOURT COPSE. The enemy then rushed across the fire of the guns towards the firing line 3rd System and the 4 guns at 1000 yds range mowed down at least several hundreds in this costly attack. Till 3.30 p.m. this battery was the sole defence of VRAUCOURT. 22,000 rounds were fired in all, mostly at massed targets at close ranges.

"B" battery was less fortunate in escaping hostile artillery fire and one gun was knocked out in the morning. At 3 p.m. large formations of the enemy were seen forming up in C.1. and coming out of ECOUST. Rapid fire was opened and both these bodies of the enemy were scattered.

About 4 p.m. the enemy commenced an advance along the ridge in C.14.b. in artillery formation. Rapid fire was again opened and the battery commander claims to have knocked out the whole party.

Excellent long range shooting was also done by "C" battery. Large bodies of the enemy moving out from ECOUST towards B.3.c d. & b. and 12.b. were scattered and the advance was checked. About 3.45 p.m. a more determined advance was made by a force estimated at about 2 battalions in open order. These waves were annihilated, except for a few survivors who could be seen running down the reverse slope of the ridge.

At 9.30 p.m. 4 new guns were received from D.A.D.O.S. and these were used to make batteries up to 5 guns per battery. Oil and ammunition were also sent up to the batteries.

At 1 a.m. 22nd inst. orders were received that the Division was being relieved by the 40th Division and that "A" Coy. which formed the garrison for "A", "B" & "C" batteries and also manned 4 guns at MORT HOMME would come under the orders of 40th Division.

The following is a summary of the report of the commander of this company.

"A" Battery   About 1 p.m. on the 22nd the officer commanding "A" battery was informed that the Pioneers who were protecting his right flank were withdrawing to dig a new trench near MORY. The Infantry who were also garrisoning the trench mistaking this for a general order to withdraw, also retired, leaving the machine guns once more the sole defence of VRAUCOURT

By 3.30 p.m. the enemy had worked round on the southern flank and one party got into the same trench within 30 yds of the guns. Bombing blocks were at once made and spare numbers engaged the enemy with bombs and rifles   Meanwhile the enemy had got in rear of the position and the teams were being sniped from behind, the subsection officer and several other ranks being wounded. Lieut. Crocker, the Section officer now decided to withdraw and the teams started off carrying their guns, kit and wounded with them. Lieut. Crocker remained behind with the gun and covered the withdrawal of the remainder. One man carrying his gun was pounced on by the Bosche and his gun was captured, but otherwise the withdrawal was effected without casualties.

-4-

The 3 guns of this battery still remaining proceeded to reinforce "C" battery.

"B" Battery. At 2.50 p.m. on the 22nd under cover of a heavy barrage the enemy commenced to work up the Firing line 3rd System from the east and our Infantry were withdrawn to the support line. 2/Lt. Brackenridge, who was in charge of the battery sent 2 guns to support the Infantry in the support line 3rd System, and mounting his remaining 2 guns on the south bank of the road he mowed the enemy down until his ammunition was exhausted and his guns were destroyed by trench mortars. 2/Lt. Brackenridge, though 3 times wounded, refused to leave and was finally carried away by his corporal.

"C" Battery. By the early evening of the 22nd the position at "C" battery had also become serious, as the Infantry on the flanks were being pushed back and the guns were in danger of isolation. The position was improved, however, by the arrival of 2/Lt. Crocker and 3 guns from "A" battery. Positions guarding the flanks were taken up and preparations for all round defence were made. Later on Lieut. Pulley, the officer in charge was informed by the officer commanding the Infantry that he had been ordered to withdraw to the next System and it was urged that the machine guns should conform. Lt. Pulley, however, volunteered to cover the withdrawal of the Infantry which was effected with slight loss. As soon as the Infantry had withdrawn the enemy launched an attack in mass; this was held in check for a considerable time and very heavy casualties were inflicted, but it was soon apparent that the enemy had established himself on the now undefended cross roads at the Sugar Factory and MORT HOMME and a withdrawal became imperative.

Orders were therefore given to withdraw to the ridge in rear. This was done in good order, guns stopping and giving covering fire to the remainder. One man only was lost during this withdrawal.

It was now decided to dispose the 8 guns remaining about B.13 & 22 for the defence of MORY but, as by this time belts and gunners had become scarce it was necessary to reserve fire for exceptional targets.

Reserve Section. The Reserve Section, which was in reserve at MORT HOMME on the morning of the 22nd also accounted for a large number of the enemy, especially in dealing with heavy attacks, between 5 & 6.30 p.m. during which time 12,000 rounds were fired at close range. At 3.30 p.m. the Infantry had completed their withdrawal from the MORT HOMME line and the officer in charge was ordered to take up a position in the Army line.

The early morning of the 23rd saw the enemy in MORY and the Company H.Q. with one gun mounted on a Mark IV tripod and 2 guns mounted on sandbags with 50 Infantry dug themselves in facing north across the valley in B.29 a. Here excellent targets were obtained, although the fullest advantage could not be taken of them owing to shortage of ammunition only 1700 rounds being fired. It was afterwards ascertained that the remaining guns had retired by stages to a position east of ERVILLERS covering the withdrawal of the Infantry each time. From these positions the enemy were again engaged with good effect though firing was greatly restricted owing to shortage of belt boxes.

On the night of 23/24th the company was relieved by a company of the 40th Division and withdrew to the ERVILLERS - BEHAGNIES line. As a precaution positions were selected and dug for the 10 remaining guns between M.1.b.00.50. and E.25.b.50.40. Touch was maintained with a Machine Gun Coy. on the left but the Coy. on the right flank could not be found.

At 10 p.m. the company limbers arrived to take the remnants of the company from the battle area. Shortly afterwards however the S.O.S. went up from ERVILLERS and it was out of the question to withdraw. Two guns were sent to the threatened flank. No action however took place though the guns were able to fire 700 rounds at good targets. About 2 p.m. the Infantry again commenced to withdraw on either side of BEHAGNIES and it was necessary for the Brigade, to which the guns were now attached, to conform.

— 59th Battn Machine Gun Corps —

Notes on German Attack — March 21st 1918.

On March 3rd the Divisional Front was reduced and extended from 400 yds North of BULLECOURT to 400 yds north of the L'Hirondelle river; the reduced frontage being rather more than 4000 yards.

The attack which developed on March 21st had been expected for some time, and the following measures had been taken by the Coys. to meet it.

1. Tunnellers had been used extensively to construct champagne emplacements. Though the programme was not carried out entirely, most of the guns had shafts 20 feet deep by the 21st.

2. A line of Emplacements known as the 'B' positions had been prepared about 3000 yds behind the firing line. The construction of dug-outs for these positions had not commenced.

3. Carefully camouflaged champagne emplacements for 3 four gun batteries had been prepared between 5,000 and 6,000 yds from our firing line.

4. Three 8 gun battery positions (X Y & Z) had been dug and stocked with ammunition to support a counter attack on the firing line of the 2nd system should this be necessary.

5. Emplacements were stocked with 15,000 rounds of S.A.A. per gun, an iron ration of oil, and water, and rations for 48 hours.

6. Practice alarms were held every 48 hours and the times taken to get into position were reported to Battn Hdqrs. The teams were also practised in firing with Box Respirators.

7. A counter-preparation programme was drawn up to be used should an attack appear imminent. Not more than 5,000 rounds per gun were to be expended on counter preparation and orders were given that no attempt should be made at long range fire should guns come under the hostile bombardment.

Dispositions.

The extent of the front made it impossible to cover the forward zone with short range m.g. fire with the guns available without sacrificing unduly the principle of defence in depth. Guns were therefore placed so as to protect the most important features, and while this increased the chances of guns being dealt with in detail by the Enemy the front was defended to a depth of about 6,000 yds.

The 64 guns were disposed approximately as follows:

Between 0 and 500 yds of firing line		2 guns.
" 500 1,000 " " "		12 "
" 1,000 2,000 " " "		14 "
" 2,000 3,000 " " "		8 "
" 3,000 4,000 (B positions)		12 "
" 5,000 6,000 (A, B & C batteries)		12 "
In Reserve 8,000		4 "
		64

The type of emplacement used was a small open emplacement designed to protect the gunners against any shelling except a direct hit. Most of the guns in the forward system were in trenches as sufficient time was not available to carry the spoil from dug-outs long distances. The emplacements of the 'B' positions which covered the support line of the 2nd system were in carefully camouflaged pits but dug-outs had not been constructed. A, B & C. Battery positions consisted of carefully camouflaged mined dug-outs with underground communication between the various guns.

A few days before the attack orders had been received to man the rear positions with nucleus teams.

As troops in the same Army had sustained casualties through prolonged gas bombardment the Corps issued orders on the 20th for gun teams to be reduced to 1 N.C.O. & 4 men in order that a relief might be available. This was done before the attack commenced.

At about 5 a.m. on the 21st the Enemy commenced a heavy bombardment and at 5.30 orders were received from the Division to assume Battle stations. The Balance of the teams for the rear positions were galloped up in the limbers and the limbers returned at 7 a.m. without casualties.

The enemy maintained a heavy bombardment of gas shells and H.E. until shortly after 9 when his infantry attacked. The main weight of the attack came up the Noreuil Valley, the defences of which had been pulverized by the preliminary bombardment, the plan being to bomb up our support and reserve trenches at the same time as frontal attacks were being delivered.

Very little has been heard of the guns in the forward system as survivors have only returned from 3 groups of guns.

The guns at 28a and 29a opened fire on S.O.S. lines, as soon as the hostile bombardment commenced, as they assumed an S.O.S. had gone up, until the guns were knocked out by shrapnel. While an effort was being made to repair the guns, the enemy advanced to within 30 yards of the gun position, and fire was opened on them with rifles and revolvers. The enemy were held up for some time, and commenced an encircling movement. The teams then withdrew, and did considerable further execution with a Lewis gun borrowed from the Artillery.

The Guns 30a and 31a were destroyed by shell fire early in the action.

A survivor from 24a and 25a states that guns opened fire on S.O.S. lines, when the bombardment commenced. About 9 a.m. the enemy appeared about 750 yards in front, and advanced to within 200 yards of the guns. During this advance the survivor states, that at least 1,000 of the enemy were killed by M.G. fire. At 12.30 P.M. the guns were destroyed by shrapnel, and the teams withdrew to the dug-out. They were then bombed from the back entrance by the enemy, and the survivor escaped through the front entrance of the dug-out.

4

Guns Nos 24-27 fired from 5 a.m. to 9 a.m. at slow rates on S.O.S. lines. When the bombardment commenced at 9-10 a.m. information was received that the Enemy had broken through and was making round the right flank. Guns were then mounted on the dug-out steps and fire was opened on the Enemy. Maps and documents were destroyed. In the meantime the Enemy had worked round to   Trench and had also begun to bomb up the Railway Reserve. Shortly afterwards the Officer in charge gave orders to destroy the guns and withdraw. One man returned.

Guns Nos 32-33 after inflicting about 100 casualties on the enemy at short range were bombed from the front and right. As their own bombs had been destroyed they could not reply and the Sergt in charge gave orders to withdraw to Railway Reserve where the survivors fought as Infantry. Our troops in Railway Reserve were soon outnumbered and outflanked and an Infantry Officer gave the order to withdraw.

No definite information has been received about other forward guns, though in several cases they were heard firing long after they were surrounded.

The line of the 'B' positions was subjected to a heavy Gas and H.E. bombardment from 5·30 a.m. onwards, but reports received at 11 a.m. show that only one gun had been destroyed and that the men were in good spirits and standing by for targets.

About noon the Enemy were seen massing in Ecoust and shortly afterwards they resumed their advance. Their first attacks were checked by fire from the B positions guns who bore the whole weight of the attack as no Infantry were available to garrison the support line 2nd system. Reports indicate that the first attack was defeated by M.G. fire and that Enemy were driven back into Ecoust.

During this attack intense fire could be heard from Guns Nos 26B & 36B. Finally, however the guns were surrounded and destroyed in detail. Two Signallers have returned from these gun teams.

At 12-45 p.m. orders were received to move up the Reserve Section to a position to defend Mort Homme. This was done and guns were in position about 2-30 p.m. At 3 p.m. the Enemy reached the wire of the firing line 3rd system but his attack on this line was repulsed.

As the situation was critical 100 partially trained men of the M.G. Battn. were formed into platoons and sent up as Infantry to hold the line

These men together with a platoon of Artillerymen work as an Infantry Coy under one of the Coy commanders until the situation was restored by the arrival of the supporting Divisions

The share in the battle taken by the guns in A.B. & C. Batteries and the Reserve Section is described in attached report by O.C. A. Coy.

Attached is also the sworn evidence given before a Court of Enquiry, which was ordered to assemble to obtain all possible information about the Battle

The evidence of No 3322 Pte MYRING as to the Enemy's attitude to our wounded is of particular importance

59th B. Machine Gun Corps

Headquarters Officers.   Appendix I.

Lieut Col. E. V. Basden.   M.C
Major J. W. Gaulden.   M.C.
Capt R. S. Simmint.   2/6 N. Staffs Regt.
Lieut & QMr H. Wright.   2/4 Lincoln Regt.
Lieut H. S. Newton.   Machine Gun Corps.
Capt H. W. Taylor.   R. A. M. C. (Attached).

– Strictly Secret –
– 59th Batt. M.G. Corps. –
– Operation Order No 2 –

Copy No II
25-3-18

Reference Sheet
Lens. 11 1/100,000.

Appendix 2.

1. The enemy is reported to have reached ERVILLERS and his cavalry are reported to be active. There is a possibility that some of his cavalry patrols may lose their way and there may therefore be a chance of obtaining captures.

2. Reference above, Capt Gardiner will picquet the following roads with a post of 1 N.C.O. 9 men and one cyclist orderly at each road.

 (a). TOUTENCOURT – VARDENCOURT. RD.
 (b). VARDENCOURT – WARLOY. RD.
 (c). VARDENCOURT – HARPONVILLE. RD.

3. Reports will be sent every two hours to these HQs.

4. The men in the HQs. billet near the main cross roads will sleep with their boots on and find a double sentry. They will be prepared to act at short notice. The R.S.M. will be in charge of this party.

5. Capt Gardiner will have his HQrs at Batt H.Qrs.

6. Acknowledge.

Issued at 10 P.M.
Copies 1-4 to Coys.
 5 Capt Gardiner.
 6 59th Division.
 7 R.S.M.
 8+9 Retained.

Capt. & Adjt.
59 Bn. M.G.C.

Reference Sheet.

— Secret —
— 59th Batt. M.G.C. —
— Operation Order No 4. —

Copy to II
Appendix 3.

LEM 11
HAZEBROUCK. 5?

1. The 59th Division (less Artillery and 177th Brigade) will be transferred to 1st Corps, First Army and will be accommodated in Northern Portion of BUSNES Area.

2. The Battalion (less A. Coy attached 177th Brigade and Transport) will move by tactical train tomorrow from CAMPAS. STN.
Time of Parade will be notified later.

3. The Transport will move by Route March on 28th and 29th under orders to be issued later.

4. All baggage and stores not carried on the train must be loaded on to Transport by 5 A.M. tomorrow morning. Separate orders have been issued regarding Officers' Valises and carriage of Camp Kettles.

5. Dress Marching Order plus one blanket to be carried on pack.
Steel helmets will be carried on pack.

6. Rations   Rations for consumption tomorrow will be issued tomorrow morning less biscuits which will be carried in bulk on train and issued at detraining station for consumption.
A fresh meat ration will be issued tomorrow morning and will be consumed tomorrow. Rations for the 29th inst less preserved meat already issued, will be issued at detraining station.
All Water Bottles must be filled from the Water Carts before 6 A.M. tomorrow morning.

7. Acknowledge.

Issued by D.R. at

Distribution Normal.

H. Lumans
Capt. & Adjt.
59th Bn. M.G.C.

Confidential

WA 2

War Diary

59th Battn Machine Gun Corps

April 1918

Pages 7-9

WAR DIARY
or
INTELLIGENCE SUMMARY

Army Form C. 2118.

APRIL 1918 Vol I Page 1

Place	Date	Hour	Summary of Events and Information	Remarks and references to Appendices
VILLERS BRULIN (Sheet LENS 11) 1/40000	1.4.18	9.15	Bn (less transport) marched to AUBIGNY STN when it entrained for PROVEN, arriving there 8.30pm. On detraining Bn marched to Camp at ST JANSTER-BIEZEN.	See Appendix 1/4/18
Sheet HAZEBROUCK S.2.A. 1/100000	2.4.18		Order received from Div. that Bn would relieve Right Battn. of 33rd Div. in the Line East of YPRES on the morning of 4/5th April 18. As many pres as possible on training.	
	3/4/18		B.G. M.G.C. G.H.Q. and D.A.M.G. visited Bn. Bn less transport inspected in Camp. Paraded by Gen. Plumer Comm'd of Second Army.	
	4/4/18	16.30	Bn less A & D Coys moved to M.G. Bn Camp at POTITZE.	} Appendix 2 W.D.2
	5/4/18		At dawn B Coy relieved one Coy of 33RD M.G. Bn in the Right Sector of 33rd Div Front with 15 guns.	
		10.00	Bn relieved 33rd Bn M.G.C. at M.G. Bn Camp POTITZE.	
Sheet 27 (France and Belgium) 1/40000	6/4/18		A & D Coys moved to new camp at L.9.b.8.5.	
	7/4/18		D Coy moved by road and rail to M.G. Bn Camp POTITZE.	
ZONNEBEKE 1/10000	8/4/18		C Coy plus 2 Sections of D Coy attached to C Coy relieved 24 guns of right M.G. Bn in the Left Sub Sector of Divisional Front. Relief being completed by 10.15 pm.	} Appendix 3 W.D.3
Sheet 28 (BELGIUM) 1/40000	10/4/18		A Coy moved forward into YPRES area being accommodated at No 1 Camp (H.17. d. 5.4) and No 15 Camp. (H.16.a.9.2)	
	12/4/18	12 midnight	A Coy moved to DRANOUTRE and proceed under the orders of G.O.C. 178 Infy Bde (Sheet 28) Bn (less A Coy) withdrew from line to RIDGE CAMP, BRANDOEK	Appendix 4 W.D.5
	13/4/18	11 a.m.	D Coy. marched to GODESWAERSVELDE (Sheet 27) and came under orders of G.O.C. 176 Infy Bde.	
		1 p.m.	Bn (less A & C Coys) entrained at BRANDOEK for GODEWAERSVELDE and marched to BERTHEN (Sheet 27) arriving there night.	

Army Form C. 2118.

WAR DIARY
or
INTELLIGENCE SUMMARY
(Erase heading not required.)

W L I Page 8. APRIL 1918

Place	Date	Hour	Summary of Events and Information	Remarks and references to Appendices
LOCRE Ref Sheet 28 Belgium 1.40,000	14/4/18	10 a.m.	C Coy marched to LOCRE (Sheet 28) and came under orders of G.O.C. 177 Infy Bde.	
		11 a.m.	Bn HQ and B Coy marched to LOCRE, passing into Divl. Reserve, and camped at SOUTH HILL CAMP M23a 2.9 (Sheet 28)	
		5pm	Officer of B. Coy reconnoitre Army Line (DRANOUTRE - METEREN LINE)	
		10pm	B. Coy relieves guns of 34"/135" M.G.C. in DRANOUTRE - METEREN LINE. Batt HQ remain at SOUTH HILL CAMP. (M23a 2.9) (Sheet 28)	
	15		Advance Bn. HQ formed with HQ. B. Cy.	
	16		Orders received that guns of B. Cy are now under 34" Division. Bde Comdr will two guns from part of composite force under Brig Sommewell Currently 177134, and men of will that Bde free	
	18		59"Div loo M.G Bn more from forward area	
	19		Orders received that all machine Guns in the Line will be relieved by hand houss on 20/21" April 15 P.P.	
	20	6pm	Bn. HQ move to GODEWAERSVELDE	
	21	6pm	B Coy relieved by hand troops from GODEWAERSVELDE & await concentration of Companies. D&C Coy report Batt. HQ. Bn HQ at GODEWAERSVELDE.	
	22		Bn HQ moved to billets S.E of HERZEELE.	
	23	2pm	A Coy open Battalion. Battalion cleaning and checking kit	Appendix 6 1/26
		9am 4p	Batt. cleaning and reorganising	
	24	am 4p	Batt. training	
	25		Batt. training. Commanding Officer reconnoitres WATOU-CAESTRE LINE	

Army Form C. 2118.

APRIL 1918

WAR DIARY
or
INTELLIGENCE SUMMARY.
(Erase heading not required.)

Vol 1. page 9.

Place	Date	Hour	Summary of Events and Information	Remarks and references to Appendices
HERZEELE	26	2p	Orders received that Battalion will stand by to move at 30 minutes notice. Orders received the Coys are detailed as follows:- A Coy to 176" Infy Bde B " to 178 " C " to 177 " " D " " " to Divisional Reserve.	Appendix 7 1/27
	27	1p	Orders received the Bn HQ and D Coy will move to Road Cross F.25.d.8.3. (Sheet 27)	
		9am	Commanding Officer reconnoitres Army Line (WATOU - CAESTRE) Major Stewart e. Coy ordered to report to 5" M.G. Bn. Lt Anderson c Coy ordered do do	
	28		Battn H Q moves to Division at H.Q. (F.22.b.1.1 Sheet 27)	
	29		Major Stewart A. Cy wounded.	
	30		Commanding Officer visits Coys attached to Bdes. Casualties in Battn for month (a) killed 3 officers 14 ORs (b) wounded 3 " 69 " (c) missing - 49 " (d) died of wounds - 1 2 6 offrs 134 ORs	

59th Divisional Troops

59th BATTALION

MACHINE GUN CORPS

APRIL 1918.

REPORT ON OPERATIONS ATTACHED.

APPENDIX I.

MACHINE GUN DEFENCE.

In the event of a serious attack, the following changes in disposition will be made :-

1. The O.C. M.G. Battn. will report to D.H.Q.

2. Advanced Battn. H.Q. will be established at L'HOMME MORT.

3. The O.C. Right Coy., with runners, will report to Right Bde. H.Q. at VRAUCOURT.

4. The O.C. Left Coy. will move to Advanced Headquarters at C.8.a.2.5. As long as communication lasts his company will be commanded by the officer in charge Advanced Battn. H.Q., who will be in close touch with the Left Brigade at L'HOMME MORT.

5. The "B" positions will be manned by a Reserve Coy. (Coy. H.Q. L'HOMME MORT).

6. A, B & C Batteries will be manned by a Reserve Coy. (Coy. H.Q. C Battery at present).

7. The remaining section of the Reserve Coy. will move up with pack animals to the Camp at B.22.b. and a runner will be sent to Advanced Battn. H.Q.

8. In the event of an attack taking place at night, or being obscured by a smoke barrage on the gun positions, guns will fire on their S.O.S. lines until it is reported that our line has been broken. Fire will then be directed on the foreground away from communication trenches until it is ascertained that our infantry have withdrawn. The guns at U.26.c.7.3. and U.27.d.2.5. will not open fire at short range without reference to the Battn. H.Q. close by.

9. Should the enemy's advance be screened by a creeping barrage consisting partly of smoke, fire will be opened at the barrage plus 150 yards range.

10. Skeleton wire will be put out at least 60 yards from each M.G. emplacement.

11. Emergency rations and water for 2 days will be kept at all forward and "A" & "B" positions.

(Sd.) R.ST.G.GORTON,
Bt.-Colonel,
G.S. 59th Division.

6/3/18.

Two guns were sent in advance to the new line and the Infantry retirement was covered by the 4 guns now remaining, 3 of which were firing back to back. Excellent targets were obtained again and heavy casualties inflicted.

By 4.30 p.m. the Infantry were in their new line and the guns which were now being shelled by our Artillery were withdrawn. On arrival at the new line good targets were again engaged with effect, e.g. 2 enemy machine guns were put out of action and a mounted Staff was dispersed.

During the night 25/26th the company was withdrawn.

The Divisional letter marked as Appendix 1 shows the dispositions adopted on the morning of the 21st.

The lessons to be learnt from the action are as follows :-

1. 64 guns capable of keeping up sustained fire are not sufficient for a Division. Had double the number of guns been available it is reasonable to suppose that the enemy would have only gone half the distance at double the cost.

2. As long as the enemy pursues his present plan of attack, i.e. to break through on a small portion of front and then to attack the remainder of our front system from a flank, it is a mistake to teach machine gunners that they have a definite front and a definite battle line. Most of the machine guns of the Division were apparently attacked from the flank or rear.

3. It is thought that greater use might have been made of the Lewis guns. Most of these had no dug-outs and doubtless many were destroyed by the initial bombardment. It is thought that if the Lewis guns had been organised into Lewis gun companies and withdrawn to the line of the "B" machine gun positions that the "B" machine guns and Lewis guns could, together, have held the enemy in check. As it was the flanks of the machine guns were in the air and they were dealt with in detail owing to their small number.

4. The enemy used more shrapnel than was anticipated. Whenever possible splinter-proof emplacements should be made.

5. The great importance of defence in depth was illustrated in the attack. The guns which held the enemy up were 6000 yds behind our firing line at zero.

6. Communication by visual was impossible owing to smoke.

7. Though orders had been given that guns should not fire while they were subjected to the hostile bombardment, except in case of S.O.S, several teams assumed that an S.O.S. had gone up when the intense bombardment started as it was impossible to see anything. Guns which might have later been used for direct fire were thus destroyed before zero

It is open to question, if a heavy attack is expected, if guns should fire on S.O.S. lines or should reserve the fire.

8. The system of maintaining guns in Army Parks worked admirably. Within 3 hours of the wire being sent to D.A.D.O.S. new guns were in action against the enemy.

9. The enormous killing power of the gun was demonstrated on many occasions.

10. Carefully camouflaged emplacements, even when these were mined dugouts, were not discovered by the enemy or interfered with by the hostile artillery.

11. To enable the gun team to be responsible for its own local protection at least 6 men are necessary.

(Sd.) E.D. BASDEN, Lt.Col.,
D.M.G.C.,
59th Division.

5/4/18.

Refce/Sheet 28 S.W.

59th Batt. Machine Gun Corps

Report on Operations April 13th – 20th 1918

The Battalion, less A Coy on being withdrawn from the YPRES salient arrived at BRANDHOEK at 4.30 am on the 13th inst. At 6 am orders were received that a Company was to move to WESTOUTRE at noon and await orders there. D Coy were detailed for this, and on arrival at WESTOUTRE were attached to 176th Brigade. The Battalion, less 2 Coys, entrained at BRANDHOEK station at 1.30 pm for GODEWAERSVELDE and bivouacked on the night 13/14th at BERTHEN. At 10.15 am orders were received that the Unit was to march at once to LOCRE and that 1 Company was to report to 177th Bde. The remaining Company was to take up a position in the DRANOUTRE-METEREN line. C Coy were detailed to report to 177th Brigade leaving B Coy with the Battalion.

The following is a summary of the part taken in the Battle by the Battalion.

<u>D Coy</u>   This Company arrived at LOCRE with the 176th Brigade at 6 am on the 14th inst. It was expected that the Brigade would be used to counter-attack any portion of the line between NEUVE EGLISE and METEREN should the Enemy gain a lodgement. Reconnaissance of the line particularly in the direction of NEUVE EGLISE was therefore made at once. One section was attached to each of the 2 Battalions detailed for the attack and the other 2 sections remained with the Battalion in support. Later orders were received that a defensive line was to be held through S.12.c.4 and this line was reconnoitred. Finally at 7 pm orders were received the ⎯⎯⎯ Brigade was to

relieve the 3 Brigades defending BAILEUL and to hold the line from S 19 to S 25. 30 machine guns were in this line belonging to 3 Coys and it was impossible to arrange a relief owing to lack of communication and the small number of guns at the disposal of the Coy Commander. Consequently the sections were moved into the line with the Battalions to which they were attached except for 1 section with the reserve Battalion which was used to form a mobile reserve near Brigade Headquarters.

Contrary to expectation the 30 guns of the relieved Brigades were withdrawn from the sector without any arrangements being made for their relief.

At 1 p.m. on the 15th the Enemy put down a heavy barrage on MONT de LILLE and the left of the Brigade Sector and at about 2 p.m. information was received that the Brigade on the left were falling back under heavy pressure. The left of the 176th Brigade became involved in this attack about 2.30 p.m. but the 4 machine guns on the left flank were able to pulverize the attack at short range and inflict very heavy casualties. As the withdrawal of the 177th Brigade proceeded it became necessary to withdraw to the Railway line running through S 21 a. By this time 2 of the four guns had been knocked out but the remaining 2 guns were got into action ~~again~~ on the Railway line and again inflicted heavy casualties on the Enemy.

On news of the withdrawal of the left Brigade being received the section in reserve

(3)

was ordered to take up a position in S.3.d. in order to cover the valley running North and South from MONT DE LILLE. These guns although the Officer & Section Sergt. were killed and the total strength was reduced to 10 remained in action five days. The whole Enemy attack swept across their front and very heavy casualties were inflicted. Smaller targets were engaged on subsequent days and every day casualties were seen to be inflicted on the Enemy.

Of the guns attached to the centre Battn. two were destroyed by shell fire early in the action and the remaining two after engaging a few good targets and covering the withdrawal of the Infantry were ordered by the OC Battn to withdraw. The guns attached to the Right Battalion, less one which was knocked out remained in position until withdrawn by the OC Battalion on the night 15/16th to conform with the general line.

<u>C Coy</u> This Company also experienced difficulties owing to the short time allowed for the relief. The Company arrived at LOCRE about mid-day on the 14th and at 5 pm the Coy. Commander received instructions to report to G.O.C. 177th Brigade at S.14.d.2.3. On reporting it was explained to him that the Brigade would probably relieve the Brigades in the line from S.18.b.9980 – S.22.c.4.3 on the night 15/16th and he was ordered to make a reconnaissance. The reconnaissance showed that 25 guns of the 23rd Battn were in the area and 10 guns of the 34th Battn. On returning to Brigade at 10 pm the Coy Comdr was informed that the relief would be carried

(2)

out at once. Guns were therefore attached to Battalions in the same way as I Coy, 10 guns being attached to the Left Battn. and 6 to the Right Battn. By dawn on the 15th the guns attached to the Right Battn were in position. The guns attached to the Left Battalion were unable to get to the positions intended in S.18 c+b owing to daylight intervening and took up a position at HALLS FARM S.23.a.86.

The 6 guns which were attached to the Right Battalion took up positions in S.22. They survived the initial barrage which opened at 2 p.m. and engaged and dispersed large bodies of the Enemy who were forming up on the road running through S.28a and S.28b. It is not clear what happened to the two guns which were on the forward slope of the hill at S.22.d.+7. but they were heard firing for a long time. The 2 guns at S.22.c.7.4 after half an hours continuous firing were destroyed by shell fire about 4 p.m. The 2 guns at S.22.b.17 found themselves isolated by 4 p.m. the Infantry having withdrawn to the line of the RAVELSBERG ROAD Shortly afterwards they were heavily engaged by Machine Gun fire from the hills in S.21.d and S.18 central and the officer ordered a withdrawal in conformity with the general line. Fresh positions were taken up on the RAVELSBERG ROAD about S.15.d and from here the enemy were engaged with good effect. Parties were dispersed on the hill in S.16.d and a further withdrawal of the Infantry was covered.

By 5 p.m. our Infantry had withdrawn to the

(5)

neighbourhood of the DRANOUTRE-METEREN line and the guns, which were in danger of being surrounded withdrew to a position in S2d which was occupied till the guns were relieved 3 days later. During this period they were able to break up a hostile attack by their fire.

The 10 guns attached to the Left Battalion were in positions in S23 d & b and at HAUS FARM. These guns played a prominent part in defeating a heavy frontal attack which was launched on this Sector about 3.30 p.m. The hostile waves were enfiladed at close range and in several cases annihilated and for 2 hours the Enemy were held in check. During this time an unsuccessful counter attack was delivered against the Enemy's position at CRUCIFIX CORNER and after the failure of this attack the Enemy advanced rapidly and almost encircled the position. The situation was also rendered critical by the fact that the Enemy had sent over an Aeroplane which, besides engaging the guns with machine gun fire dropped lights on the position so enabling the hostile Artillery to draw back and intensify their barrage. All available belt fillers were collected and turned into Infantry and a great effort, unfortunately unsuccessful, was made to save the left flank. Belt boxes were now running short and the Enemy, having achieved success on the left, were threatening the rear. A withdrawal was decided upon, which, though carried out in an orderly fashion proved costly, 3 guns and 30 men being lost. The surviving teams took up a position about S8a and a

(6)

further effort was made to defend the left flank. This was successful for only a short time as belt boxes were not available in sufficient quantities and a further withdrawal took place to S.2.d.55 where the guns remained in action till relieved 3 days later.

B. Coy This Coy took up its positions in the DRANOUTRE - METEREN line which ran approximately through S8b, S2a, S4 and S5. Guns were in position by the morning of the 15th and were not involved in the Battle which took place that day. About 9.30 a.m. on the 16th the Enemy resumed the attack and directed a heavy barrage on to the area of the gun positions in S.4 & 5 by means of low flying aeroplanes. One gun was destroyed during this bombardment. The Enemy also attempted a strong attack from the asylum but were beaten off by the Infantry of the 34th Division. This Coy had not many opportunities to inflict casualties on the Enemy though they were subjected to a heavy strain being 6 days in the line under very heavy Artillery fire.

(7)

<u>A. Coy</u>   This Company had not moved with the Battalion to YPRES and had been attached to the 178th Brigade for some days and on the 12th April moved with that Brigade to the KEMMEL Area, where they remained until 13th inst. On the 13th the situation round NEUVE EGLISE being rather obscure one section of 4 guns were attached to and moved off with 7th Sherwood Foresters who were detailed to clear up the situation. NEUVE EGLISE was found to be in the hands of a battalion of Yorks and Lancs and the section remained in reserve about the railway in T.2 and T.3 with the 7th Sherwood Foresters.

During the morning the remaining three sections took up Reserve Positions on MONT KEMMEL, the Company Commander forming his H.Q. with 178th Brigade H.Q. at N.26.b.6.1.

The line from T.10.c.0.7. to T.11.a.0.0. was held by the 5th Sherwood Foresters and four guns were sent up about 1 p.m. to support this battalion. Positions were taken up about T.10.c.5.0 and T.10.c.0.7.

The remaining 2 sections on MONT KEMMEL were placed to protect the reserve line running along Regent Street through LINDENHOEK and in front of MONT KEMMEL that line being occupied by 6th Sherwood Foresters.

Until the afternoon of the 1st inst no Enemy action developed but about 5 p.m.

(8)

after a heavy bombardment NEUVE EGLISE was occupied by the enemy. During this time the enemy shell fire was heavy on all the forward system.

Owing to the fall of NEUVE EGLISE it was decided to fall back on a line running through T.2 c & d, T3 c & d, T+ b to Durham Road. At 12.30. am. 14/15th April 4 guns moved to a line W.33 c 30, 80, 42 90 to cover the valley in T2d and T3c. Two guns remained in T.6 c 1 9 and 2 near GABLE Fm in T.4 b where they moved to on night 13/14th.

At dawn on the morning of the 15th owing to the left flank of the Brigade being exposed two guns under Lieut. Day moved up and kept the gap under fire until closed by our Infantry unfortunately during this operation Lieut. Day was killed.

Later it was decided to withdraw the line again to the REGENT ST - KEMMEL line the withdrawal being successfully carried out on the night of the 15th/16th assisted by covering fire of the reserve machine guns.

On the 16th at 3.30 pm orders were received that the French with the 9th Division would attack WYTCHAETE and SPANBROKENMOLEN at 6 pm. This attack was assisted by a 10 gun M.G. barrage from T.3c to T.3d in which 10.000 rounds were fired.

About 7.30 am on the morning of the 17th the enemy attempted a frontal attack on KEMMEL HILL, but completely broke down under the fire of the Infantry and Machine Guns.

(9)

In spite of the intense enemy shelling, harassing fire on the enemy was kept up all day, and many good targets were obtained by the guns. During the day 2 guns were put out of action by shell fire, but a gun of another unit was found and put into action.

All roads and valleys likely to be used by the enemy were harassed continually during the night of the 17/18th. The Company were relieved by the French on the night of 18/19th.

Lessons Learnt

1. A small Infantry Escort of picked men should be attached to each pair of guns. When guns have to hang on to the last to cover a withdrawal it is very hard for the teams to fight their way back and at the same time carry guns and belt boxes. This has too often resulted in belt boxes not being available when fresh positions are taken up.

2. During the present stage of the War special attention must be paid to training in use of ground and cover. Men fresh out from England have little or no knowledge of this.

3. When siting guns special attention should be paid to valleys and sunken roads. Valleys running behind and parallel to our front line require as much attention as valleys at right angles to it.

4. Difficulties were experienced & owing to the fact that a small scale map (1/40,000) was the only one available for issue. The use of fighting maps cannot be too strongly recommended.

5. During the present stage of semi-open warfare it has proved adviseable to attach Sections to Battns. This has proved satisfactory except that it has tended to reduce the depth of the defence. It is suggested that where this is necessary a subsection should be attached to each of the line holding Battalions, 2 Sections should be attached to the support Battn. and the remaining Section should be at the disposal of the Brigadier.

Appendix 1   59th Battn Machine Gun Corps

Copy No. 7

Operation Order No 5

Refce LENS Sheet 11
1/100,000   31.3.18.

1. The 59th Division (less Artillery & Div Transport) will move to-morrow April 1st to the Second Army

2. The Battn. (less Transport) will march to-morrow to AUBIGNY STN and entrain there for PROVEN at 12 noon.

3. <u>Order of March</u>   HQ. A. B. C. & D Coys.

4. <u>Starting Point</u>   Cross Roads facing Bn. Orderly Room. H.Q. and Coys. will pass starting point at the following times:—

     H.Q.   9.15 am.
     A   9.16 am
     B   9.17 am
     C   9.18 am
     D   9.19 am

5. <u>Route</u> Cross roads 1¼ mile S of S in SAVY then follow road running due east to AUBIGNY STN.

6. <u>Headquarters</u> Bn. Hdqrs. will close at VILLERS BRULIN at 9.0 am and

reopen on arrival in new area.

<u>Note</u> The men of the draft will parade with H.Q. under orders of Sgt Major.

INSTRUCTIONS.

1. <u>Reveille</u> 6.30 am. Breakfast 7.30 am. to-morrow morning.

2. <u>Dress</u> Marching Order plus 1 blanket. Soft caps will be worn.

3. 4 lorries will report at QrMr Stores at 7am to-morrow. Of these 1 will be sent to entrance to Chateau at 8.30 am. for H.Q. baggage & stores. 1 will be sent at same time to collect stores & baggage from each Coy Hdqrs.
2 will remain at QrMr Stores.
All baggage & stores must be loaded on to lorries directly they arrive. When lorries are loaded they will be sent back to QrMr stores.

4. <u>Loading Party</u> A loading party of 1 N.C.O. & 12 men will be sent by Sgt Major to QrMr at 7am to-morrow morning. This party, after having breakfast, will proceed on lorries to AUBIGNY STN. where they will offload stores under supervision

of RQMS.

Issue at 8.30pm by DR
Distribution - Normal

[signature]
Capt & Adjt.
59th Bn M.G.C.

SECRET   59th Bn Machine Gun Corps   Appendix 2

Operation Order No. 6   Copy No.

Ref:. Sheet 28 /40.000
Belgium & France
ZONNEBEKE 28 NE 1/10000
Ed. 10A.   3/4/18.

1/ The Battalion and No 5 Section Divl Signal Coy (less A & D Coys) will relieve the 33rd Bn M.G.C. in the PASSCHENDAELE sector at dawn on 5th Apl.

2/ B Coy will take over the positions of 1 Coy of 33rd Bn M.G.C. in the line.
C Coy will be in reserve at Battn H.Q at POTIJZE.

3/ The Battn (less A & D Coys) transport & No 5 Section Divl. Signal Coy.) will parade at 4.30 p.m. tomorrow and on arrival at QUINTIN Stn (G.7.b.7.0) will entrain at 6.15 p.m for YPRES, arriving there about 8.15 p.m.

4/ On arrival at YPRES guides from 33rd Bn M.G.C. will meet the train, and the Battn. will march to POTIJZE CAMP.

5/ All transport, including officers chargers (less A & D Coys authorized transport and 2 G.S. Wagons under Lieut. Bryce) plus No 5 Section Divl. Signal Coy. and Bn H.Q. signal cyclists will proceed to the new Battn camp at POTIJZE by march route.
Parade 10.30 a.m tomorrow at Bn H.Q
Route POPERINGHE — YPRES — MENIN GATE

6. Dress Marching Order —
Blankets will be given in to Qr Mr Stores by 7.30 a.m tomorrow

7. Rations The unconsumed portion of to-morrow's rations will be carried on the man
In addition all ranks of B Coy will carry rations for consumption on 5th inst.
All water bottles must be filled before leaving

8. Transport arrangements on arrival at YPRES will be notified later

- 2 -

8. The Transport officer will send all H.Q. Transport to Battn H.Q. at 9.30 a.m. to-morrow.
All transport of B & C Coys will be sent to their respective Coy. H.Qrs by 9 a.m.
A Baggage Wagon will be sent to Orlr Stores at 9 a.m. This must contain transport stores of B & C Coys

9. All Maps, Defence Schemes, Trench Stores & Emergency rations will be taken over from 33rd Bn M.G.C.
Copies of Stores taken over together with report on condition of Emergency rations taken over will be sent to Bn. H.Q. by 6 p.m. 5th inst.

10. The following personnel will remain behind with A & D Coys

   Major J. to Garden + batman
   Asst. Adjt   + batman
   Sergt Murdon
   Pte Penness

11. Battn H.Q. will close at ROAD CAMP at 4.30 p.m. and reopen same hour at POTIJZE CAMP.

12. Acknowledge.

Distribution
 Normal + 1 copy to 33rd Bn M.G.C.

        J.H. Sument
        Capt & Adjt
        59th Bn M.G.C.

Appendix 3

Fifth Machine Gun Corps

Operation Order No 7

Refer: Map ZONNEBEKE
28 NE /10000.

B.4.18.

1. (a) Under orders from VIII Corps the 2nd Inf Bde 1st Division and 24 machine guns of 1st M.G. Battn will relieve the 88th Inf Bde and similar number of machine guns in the right sub-sector of the 29th Divisional front on night of 7/8 April.

   (b) The 122nd Inf Bde and 24 machine guns of 41st M.G. Battn will temporarily be attached to 59th Division from 10 a.m. April 8th from which hour the G.O.C. 59th Division will resume command of the whole Divisional front from D.29.d.40.85 to D.6.d.80.35.

   (c) The 122nd Inf Bde and machine guns of 41st M.G. Battn while attached to 59th Division will be administered by 41st Division.

2. The 59th Machine Gun Battn will be prepared to relieve the 24 guns of 41st M.G. Battn on night of 8/9th April.

3. 'C' Coy plus 2 Sections of D Coy which will be attached to 'C' Coy will relieve the 24 guns of 41st M.G. Battn before dawn on 9th April 1918.

4. The details of relief will be arranged direct between O.C. 'C' Coy and O.C. Coys of 29th Division concerned.

5. Completion of relief will be notified to Bn H.Q. by code word "Hodson".

6. All Trench Stores, Reserve ration, Defence Scheme and Maps will be taken over and list of same forwarded to Bn H.Q. by 6 p.m. 9th inst.
   Map references of Gun positions will be stated.

7. The details of B and C Coys left behind in the Camp will be attached to D Coy for training.

(2)

8. The details of "C" Coy left behind (less Officers Or Mrs. Stores) will be accommodated on the NORTH side of the YPRES-POTIJZE Rd.

9. "D" Coy (less 2 sections) will be accommodated on the N side of the YPRES-POTIJZE Rd.
"D" Coy will take over H.Q. of "C" Coy on vacation by "C" Coy.

10. Acknowledge.

Issued by D.R. at 9 a.m. 8th inst

Distribution   Normal
+ Copy No 14 to 29th Bn M.G.C.
  "   "   15 - 41st Bn M.G.C.

M. Lument
Capt & Adjt.
59 Bn M.G.C.

Secret.   59th Battn. M.G.C.   Copy No. 1

Appendix 4.   Warning Orders No 1

Refce Sheet.   12/4/18
Belgium 28.
_____

1.   Orders are expected for a withdrawal to the Army Battle Zone. In the event of this occurring the 59th Division will move into Corps Reserve.

2.   The 41st Division will to-day take over the Battle Zone with the 122nd Inf Bde, 2 Battalions in Brigade Reserve and the Machine Guns at present in YPRES.

3.   The 2 guns of "D" Coy. now at POTSDAM will on relief rejoin Battn. H.Q. Transport required for this will be notified to Battn. H.Q. stating time.

4.   Companies in the forward system will to-day collect as much S.A.A., stores and Reserve Rations as possible in places to which transport is accessible. The number of belt boxes with each gun is to be reduced to 8, the remainder will be sent back to Coy. H.Q.

5.   (a)   The full amount of Mobilization Stores must be kept brought back to Battn. H.Q.

      (b)   All other SAA., stores and reserve rations collected will be sent back to CAMBRIDGE DUMP and handed over to the Divisional Bombing Officer, receipts being taken.

      (c)   Coys will notify Battn H.Q. in writing by 4 pm to-day the amount of transport they require for (a) and (b) separately.

      (d)   Guides are to be sent out to-day to learn the routes to the different dumps made so that they can guide transport when it arrives to-night as far as possible.

6.   Great care is to be taken that no abnormal movement takes place during the day which might give the enemy any idea that a withdrawal is contemplated.

7.   The subject of this orders is not to be mentioned or discussed on the telephone.

8.   Acknowledge.

Issued at 8.am by DR   M. Dumont
Distribution. Normal   Capt & adjt
                                                    59 Bn M.G.C.

SECRET   Appendix 5   59th Bn. M.G.C.

Operation Order No 8

12-11-18

1. In continuation of 59th Bn. M.G.C. Warning Order No 1, the 123rd Inf. Bde. will to-night relieve the 4 front Companies of each of the 176th and 177th Inf. Bdes. with its Hdqrs. either at the present H.Q. of 177th or 176th Inf. Bdes.

2. The Support Battalion and Reserve Coys. of the 176th Inf. Bde. will as soon as it is dusk withdraw to POTIJZE Camps.

   The 4 Reserve Companies of the 177th Inf. Bde. and the Battalion at present holding the Bristle Zone of the Divisional Reserve Line will withdraw at dusk to BRAKE CAMP.

3. All Machine Guns of B, C and D Coys (less the 2 guns of D Coy being relieved today by 41st Battn. M.G.C. at POTSDAM) will be withdrawn from the line by 10 p.m. to-night.

4. On withdrawal Coys. will march to Battn. Hdqrs. arriving there ~~after 11.30 p.m.~~ in time to parade as in para 5.

5. Trains leave SAVILLE ROAD STN (near Bn. Hdqrs) at

   No 1. Train   12 midnight   and
   No 2.   "   12.30 a.m.

   They are allotted as under:-

   No 1 Train   B Coy (less Transport)
                 D " (1 Officer, 70 OR)

   No 2 Train   C Coy (less Transport)
                 Balance of D Coy (less transport)
                 Battn Hdqrs (less transport)

   Personnel for the above trains will parade between Battn Hdqrs and Transport lines at 11.30 pm and 12 pm respectively. One guide will report to each Coy from Battn Hdqrs to guide them to the Station

- 2 -

TRANSPORT.

The following Transport will report to Coys to-night at times stated.

B. Coy. at Advanced H.Q.   13 limbers at 6 p.m.
C. Coy. at Coy Ration Dump *   ...   ...   6 p.m.
D. Coy. at B. Coy Adv. H.Qrs.   5   ...   6 p.m.

* Includes 6 for attached Sections of D Coy.

Note. D Coy will send a guide to meet their 5 limbers at B Coy Advd. H.Qrs at 6 p.m.

6. All transport must first be used for Mob. Stores, and any further stores will be then loaded on. The latter will be off loaded on the way down at CAMBRIDGE DUMP.

7. Transport on return from the line will pull at Bn. H.Q. and await orders from Lieut. Hawlins.

8. Teas will be provided at new Camp on retirement.

9. Acknowledge.

Issued by D.R. at 6 p.m.   [signature]
                                                            Capt & Adjt.
Distribution: NORMAL.   5/7 Bn. 1st R.E.

Appendix 6   59 Bn Machine Gun Corps   Copy No 12

Operation Order No 9.

Ref. Sheet 27.

(1). The 59th Bn. M.G. Corps (less 1 Coy) will move to-day by march route to the area S.E. of HERZEELE where it will be billetted.

(2). <u>Order of March</u>. H.Q. B. C and D Coys, Transport.

(3). <u>Starting Point</u>. X Roads by Bn. H. Qrs. intervals of 100 yds between Coys, and 15 yds between each 6 Vehicles will be maintained. Headquarters to pass starting point at 2 pm.

(4) <u>Route</u>. GODEWAERSVELDE — STEENVOORDE — WINNEZEELE — New Camp.

Instructions

(1) Dinners at 12.30 pm.
(2) <u>Dress</u>. Marching Order, ~~plus one Blanket~~ Soft Caps will be worn.
    Fighting Order for men of B Coy who left the line last night.
(3) Billetting party, consisting of a representative from Bn H. Qrs, Each Coy & Bn Transport will leave at 11 am to arrange billetts in the new area.
(4) Marching Out states & cleanliness of billetts certificates will be handed to the Adjutant at 1.45 pm.
(5) Each Coy will detail an orderly to report to Sgt Wagstaff at 1.50 pm. A Bn H.Q Runner will be attached to each Coy at the same time.
(6). Blankets will be carried under Coy arrangements.
(7) Acknowledge.

21st/April/1918.

W. J. Hawkes
Capt. & Adjt
59th Bn. M.G. Corps

Appendix 7

59th Bn M.G.C. Order No. 10
Refs Sheet 27   Copy No.
                                 28-4-18

1. The Battn will move to-night to the
   ST JAN TER BIEZEN area.
2. STARTING POINT   D 18 b 15
3. TIMES of starting
   A Coy   to pass starting point at 7.30 pm
   C Coy   "   "   "   "   " 7.35 "
   Bn.H.Q & D Coy "   "   "   "   " 7.40 "
   B Coy   "   "   "   "   " 7.45 "

4. Coys will march independently, and will
   be attached to Bdes as follows, to
   whom they will report on arrival.
   A Coy to 176 Bde at SCHOOL Camp
   C Coy " 177 "   " L 11 b
   B Coy " 178 "   " ROAD Camp

   Bn H.Q and D Coy will be accommodated
      at ROAD Camp

5. Acknowledge.

                          W J Hawker
                          Capt & Adjt
                     59th Bn. M.G. Corps

20/6.G.
1-5-18.

59th Bn.M.G.Corps.

      With reference to your No. G/98 of 27/4/18, herewith 8 copies of your Report on Operations April 13th - 20th, as requested.

                                      Lieut. Colonel,
1-5-18.   G.S. 59th Division.

H.Q.
59th Div.

G/98

Herewith Report on Operations of this unit called for in your office No 20/6 G dated 21.4.18

    Can eight copies be type-written & returned, please.

27/4/18.
                W.J. Fawkes Capt
                for Lt Col.
            Commanding 59th Bn M.G.C.

www.ingramcontent.com/pod-product-compliance
Lightning Source LLC
Chambersburg PA
CBHW081454160426
43193CB00013B/2476